To Bronxy, Beckem, and Shay

This book is dedicated to my beautiful, energetic grandson, Bronx. As in the book, you will learn that I affectionately call him "Bronxy."

He is the love of my life!

He makes us all laugh and has taught us how to love unconditionally.

I would also like to dedicate this book to my adorable nephew, Beckem, and my heavenly cousin, Shay, who have also blessed our lives with their Down Syndrome.

Inclusion is now, and will always be, the answer.

Text and illustrations copyright ©Heidi Brooks 2024.
First published worldwide in digital and paper editions 2024.
The author asserts the moral right to be identified as the author of this work.
All rights reserved.
No part of this publication may be stored in a retrieval system
or transmitted in any form or by any means,
electronic, mechanical, photocopying, recording or otherwise
without the prior permission of the author.

In a city just like yours, lives a little boy named Bronx.
His Gammy calls him Bronxy. He is 5 years old with chestnut-brown hair. His eyes are big and almond shaped with little flecks of honey. He has short, chubby fingers and extra wide feet.

Bronx has a dad, mom, and an older brother and sister. He loves to do all the things that you love to do.

He loves to watch movies and dance to all his favorite songs. He has some pretty good dance moves.

He has his Gammy in stitches when he tries to tickle her.

Bronx loves to play outside. Sometimes he turns on the water hose and squirts everyone. He loves to play with his cousins and always makes them laugh.

Bronx waves at every person he sees in the grocery store. Sometimes he even asks for hugs.

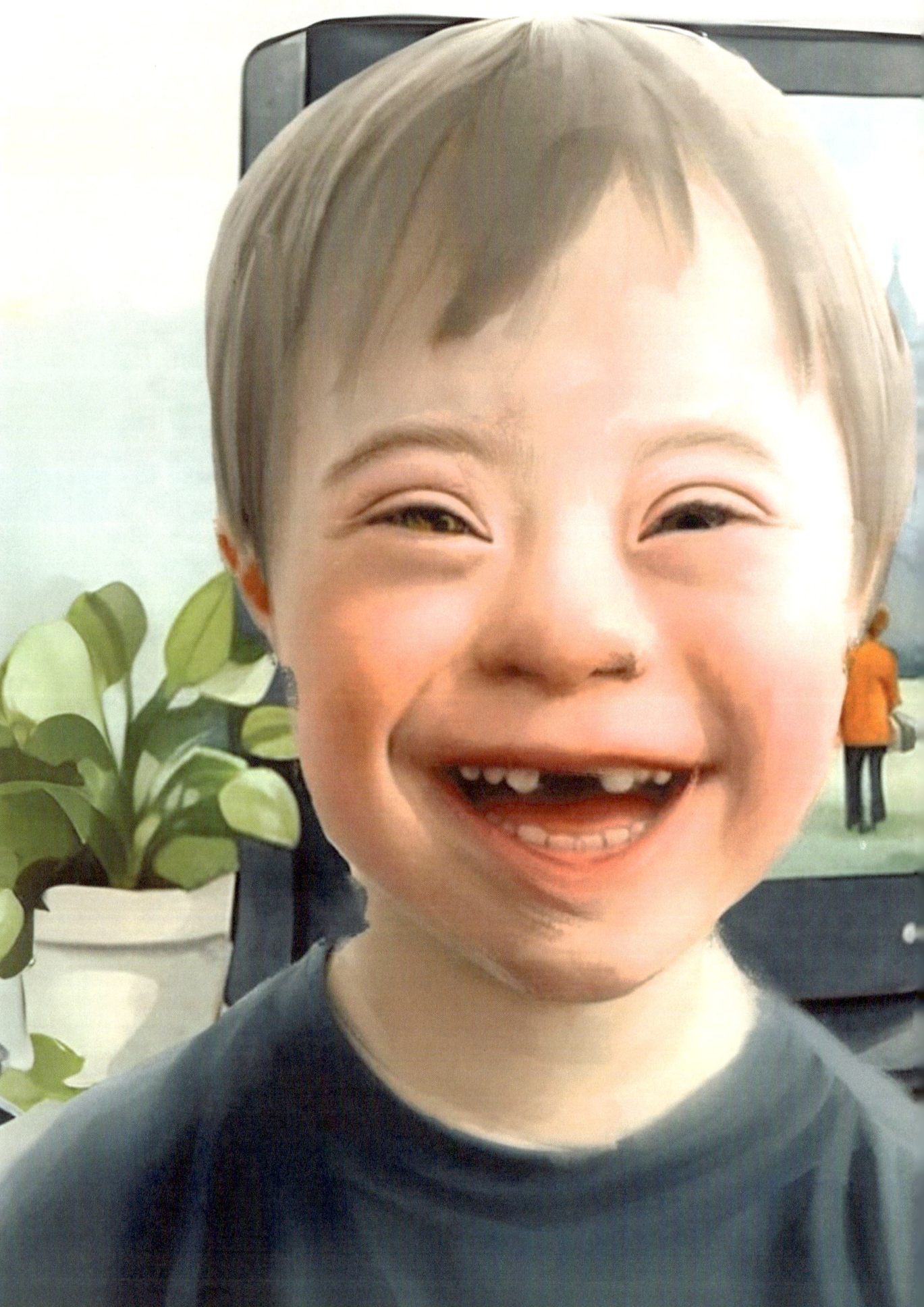

But the best part about Bronx is his smile. He will always give you a big, toothy grin — without his two front teeth, of course! His family feels very lucky to have him as their little boy.

One thing that makes Bronx special is that he has Down Syndrome. Do you know what Down Syndrome is? Well, let me tell you about it...

Most babies are born with 46 chromosomes, but a baby with Down Syndrome has an extra one. You may wonder what a chromosome is. A chromosome is one of the things that make us who we are.

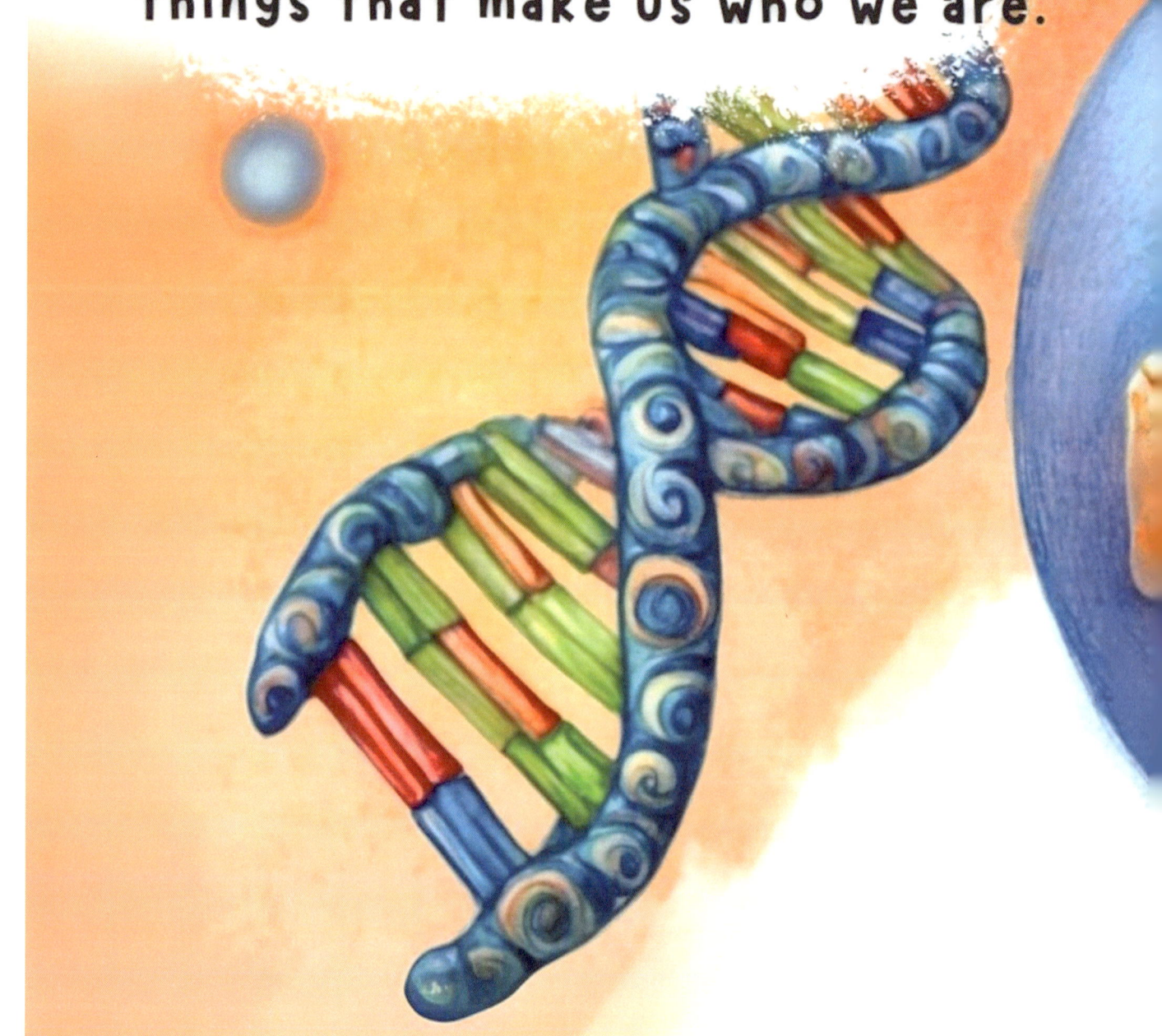

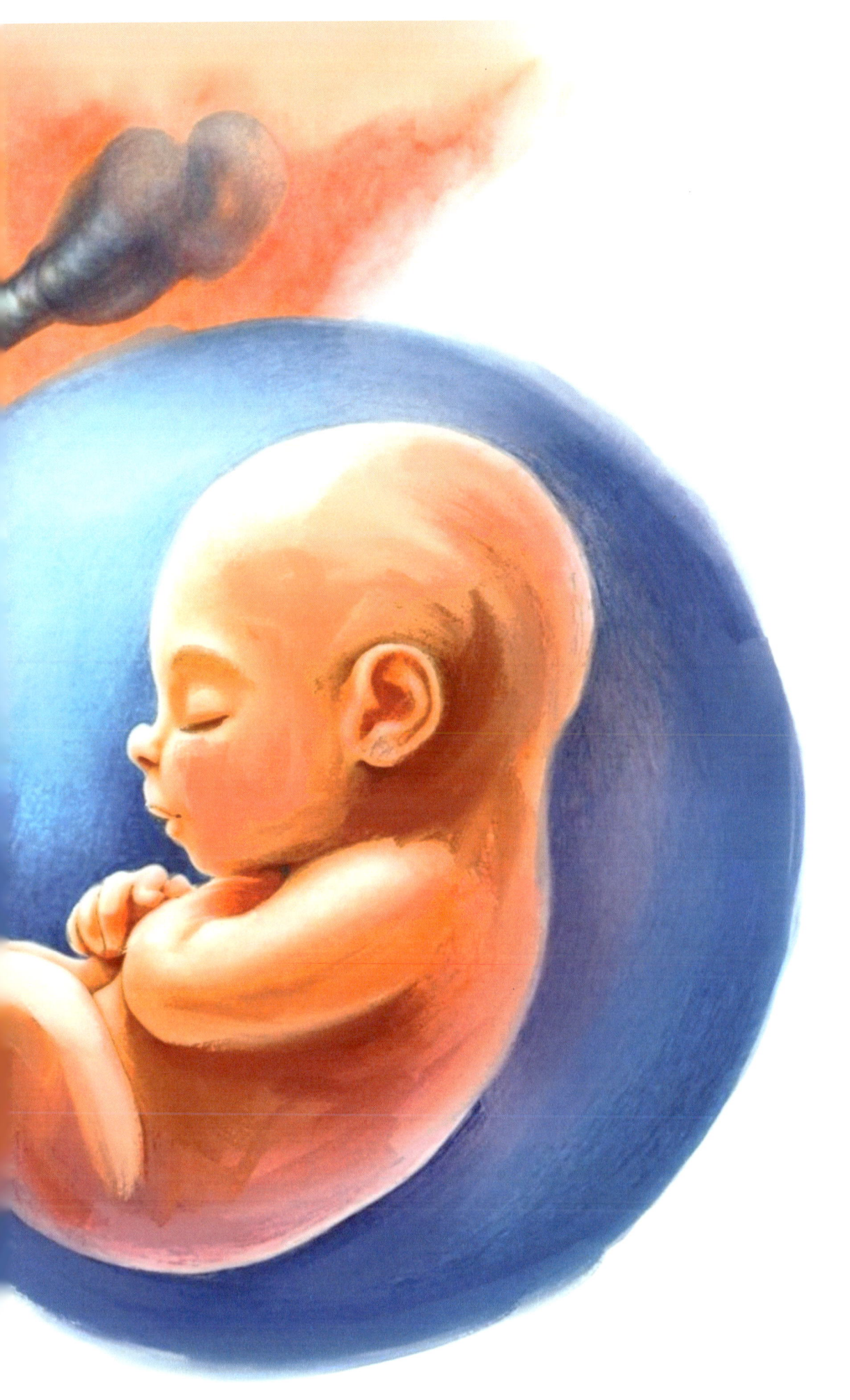

People with Down Syndrome are just like us. They laugh, eat, sleep and play.

They go to school, and when they are older, some of them go to work. They like to spend time with the people they love.

They get scared, happy, sad, and sometimes they cry, just like you and me. Sometimes it takes people with Down Syndrome a little longer to learn things. Bronx is still learning too.

When Bronx gets his haircut, he is still learning how to hold still. But he always tells everyone how handsome he is when the haircut is over.

On occasion, he will hug someone a little too tight. His dad makes him say "sorry." Bronx will learn as he gets older, just like you.

Like many kids, Bronx has a lot of fun adventures!

He loves to pretend that he is a character from the movie he is watching. He uses anything he can find in the house for his props. This always makes his sister giggle!

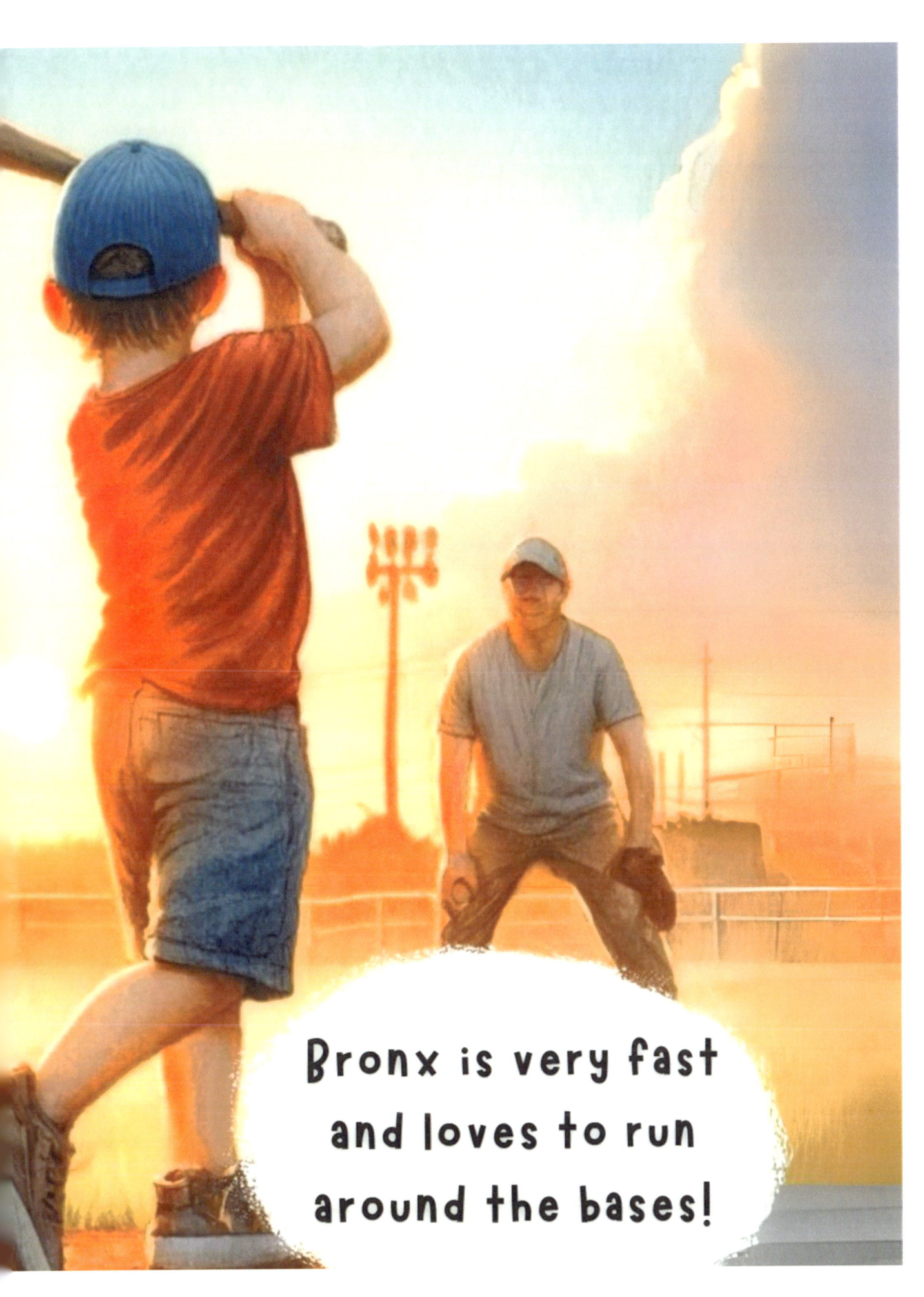

Bronx would go swimming every day if he could. Sometimes he doesn't close his eyes and drinks the water even when he is told not to. Swimming makes him very tired. His mom loves when he snuggles her until he falls asleep. She says that is the only time he holds still.

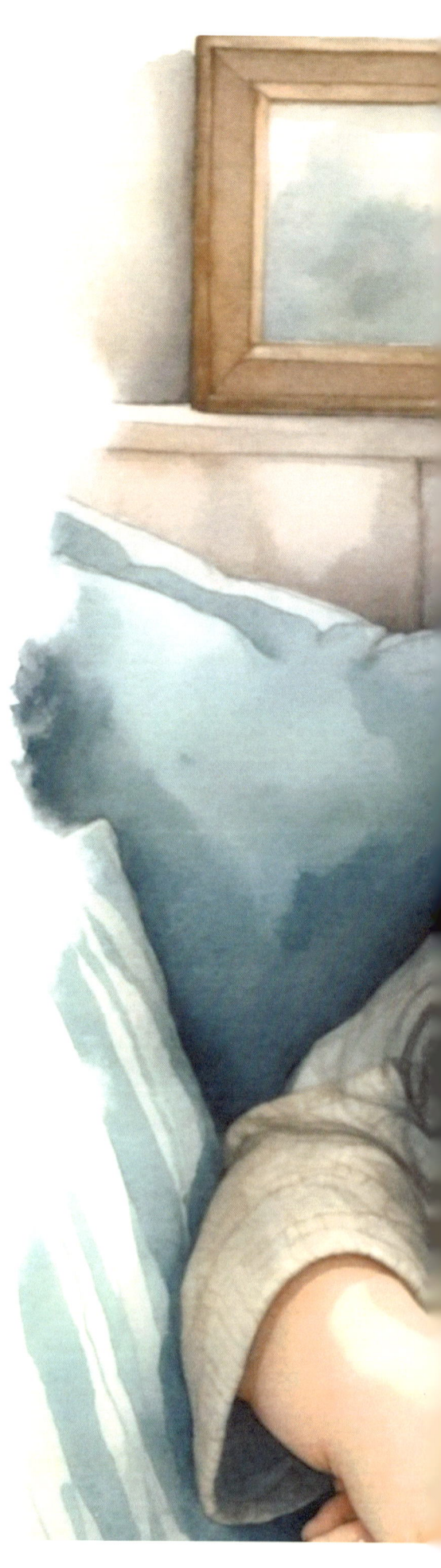

He likes to play dress up, go for rides, play with dinosaurs, and jump on the trampoline. He loves to try new adventures every day. You see, people with Down Syndrome love to do all the things we love to do.

If you see someone with Down Syndrome, say "hi" and give them a big smile. You can even invite them to play with you. You won't regret it... I promise!

Gammy & Bronx
2024

www.ingramcontent.com/pod-product-compliance
Lightning Source LLC
LaVergne TN
LVRC091353060526
838201LV00019B/292